For Judith,

Wishing you peace on
your life's journey.

Rosa Bey

June 14, 2009

AWAKENING

TO THE

PEACE WITHIN

THE JOURNEY OF SPIRIT INTO MATTER

Poems by ROSA BERGOLA

FEATHER PRESS

MONTREAL QUEBEC CANADA

Published by Feather Press

Cover Design, Manolex Design
Cover Photograph by Andrew Coulson: www.ryburnimageworks.co.uk
Author's Photograph by Grafica Foto Shoppe
Feather Motif by Donna Shvil

Legal Deposit, 2009, Bibliothèque Nationale du Québec, National Library of Canada

Printed and bound in Canada

Library and Archives Canada Cataloguing in Publication

Bergola, Rosa, 1958-
     Awakening to the peace within : the journey of spirit into matter / Rosa Bergola ; editor: Vicki Gentler.

Poems.
ISBN 978-0-9738842-0-3

     1. Peace of mind--Poetry.
I. Gentler, Vicki, 1950- II. Title.

PS8603.E685A93 2009   C811'.6   C2009-901113-1

Copies of this book may be obtained through:
Feather Press: 1-866-251-1511; 514-251-1511

Dedication

For my father
Umberto Bergola (1928 - 2005)
with deep love and gratitude
"Ci vediamo quando stiamo inseime."
"Until we see each other when we are together again."

Acknowledgements

To my mother, Elena Di Girolamo with love, respect and gratitude, you travelled thousands of miles to bring me to my home in Canada. To Jane Ely, Dean and Co-founder of The Peacemaker School, your integrity, endless support, professionalism, mentoring, teaching and especially your presence, thank you from the bottom of my heart, you are truly a living example. To Vicki Gentler, my editor, dear friend and soul sister, your ability to hold this work with honour has touched me deeply. To Christina Manolescu, Founder of the Invisible Cities Network, for your endless help and support through the self publishing process, your commitment to the self publishing community is remarkable.

To the community at The Peacemaker School, without your support this book would not have been born. To all my teachers those that are still with us and those that have moved on to the Spirit world. To all the students, clients and challenge teachers that have crossed my path, thank you for being a mirror so that I could look deeper into myself in order to deepen my awareness. To my sisters and friends who bring diversity into my life, a big thank you. Last but by no means least to Susan Pietrocatelli my life partner of 30 plus years for your tremendous love, patience and support every day and especially through the process of writing this book.

TABLE OF CONTENTS

I. DEATH

II. REMEMBERING

III REBIRTH

IV. COMING HOME

A Personal Foreword: My Inner Peace Journey

The unfolding process of peace is like the birth of a flower, beginning with the seed planted deep into the earth, the journey of finding the light, the growth and opening of petals toward sky and sun, and finally being reabsorbed back into the earth. The process occurs over and over again as it does in our own lives. My poetry is my unfolding process as a peacemaker. My poetry is the manifestation of how the principles of peacemaking have informed and changed my life.

As I made my decision to go on this journey I engaged my spirit to begin to come home to my body. In the process I found the union of matter and spirit occurred, and the essence of who I truly am came forth. In these moments, words flowed out of me effortlessly and all of my poetry came pouring through.

My experience of this process will unfold in each chapter. I feel like a seed planted deep into the darkness of death, waiting for the sparks of remembering and allowing the brilliant light of rebirth to enter my soul. In order to continue to grow my soul, I needed to go through each principle of peacemaking as it related to finding my own inner peace. These principles are community, cooperation, nonviolence and witness.

On a personal level community has been about reconnecting to my own inner voice, wisdom and intuition; a coming into communion with myself, rather than communing with the outside world. Without this inner connection I could not receive support from the people in my immediate community. I would have facilitated the process of my growth, but I would not have come to a deep understanding.

My body has always guided my life. My experience has always come first into the physical, I knew things by how my body felt. The next step was the information that came through, first in feelings, thoughts and then in words. The way this occurred in my brain was in waves of overwhelm. Everything backed up in my brain and sorting anything out seemed impossible. There was absolutely no order to the words or information. The interesting thing about all this is that I am fascinated by words, their meaning and how they come together so beautifully sometimes.

The skills I learned as a peacemaker have allowed me to sort things out. When I get overwhelmed, I have learned to take myself to meditation in my heart. The breath allows everything to slow down and I can begin to feel calm and peaceful inside. Only in this space can I focus and listen to my inner voice, and then I can identify my needs.

By going on this journey I have deepened my understanding and integrated my sense of inner peace. For me the inner peace journey is the first step into a larger life of active peacemaking in the world. I am an active Peacemaker when Spirit united with my physical form. When the union occurs a poem is created. I continue to allow old patterns and beliefs to die. I create space so that I remember who I really am. Then as each poem emerged I begin to come down the birth canal to be born again to myself. I feel a very deep expansion in this process.

When I write poetry, I feel a rush of energy swirling through my body and at that moment all is met inside. My spirit fills my body, the chatter in my mind stops and there is stillness, a kind of peacefulness that occurs the same way it does before any moment of birth. I experience the same thing when I take a walk in the woods. There is so much stillness before you hear a sound. It is really in the peacefulness of my life when I can create poetry, everything has to come to a stop, and then I can allow the inner dance to occur. The preverbal and nonlinear parts of myself need space and time before my own creative flow of writing poetry can become manifest. My soul has grown every time I watch parts of myself die and then be reborn in a new way. The creative force engages the remembering of my cellular body and then I can remember who I really am. I can manifest or give birth to the part of myself that has been repatterned. At this point the soul is initiated and begins to grow.

I
DEATH

THE RETURN

Enter the doorway
of grief
at the center
of the vortex
where death
and rebirth
occurs
in every cell of
your body

Like everyone
and everything,
Have you forgotten
the whirl-wind of
your grief?

Have you forgotten?
The winds of change
are upon you.

Take a breath!

Is it not difficult,
the last one?

To love is to laugh
and to shed tears.

Without tears
there is no cleansing,
the water cannot
cleanse us.

Call upon the tears
let them wash away
all that you are,
let go—

Let the Great Mother
hold you—

Allow each tear's
transformation
into the golden light
of the Father
as it touches the
Earth.

Let the breath
stand still.

Listen to your heart.

You have arrived!!!!

You have arrived!!!!!!

I AM

I AM
THE LIGHT
THE RESURRECTION

I AM
THE BREATH
OF ALL LIFE

I AM
ALL THAT
EXISTS
AND I AM

I AM
THE ESSENCE
OF A DROP OF RAIN

I AM EVERYWHERE

I AM ALWAYS ALIVE

I AM

I AM

I AM ALL

SACRED LAND

I walked upon the
road one day.

I walked upon the
road

I walked

The night was as
still as the air

Death came upon
me like a soft
blanket of snow.

I saw my footsteps
and I remembered

I remembered where
I had come from
and
where I was going.

This my friend felt
like a breath of fresh
air.

The journey began
I am walking to a
sacred land.

ALIVE!

There is
a feeling in my
heart.

A feeling of nothingness.

I thought this was
emptiness
but it was not.

Instead the feeling is
one we all live
with eventually.

This, my dear one, is
of death.

The illusions and the
images are dying.

Who I was is
no more.

All of our senses
are wrapped up
in death.

I didn't know
what it was.

Now I can feel
all of it.

The funny thing is
this death
is inevitable.

To invite death is
to invite the birth
of remembering who
we truly are.

Remembering why we
are here.

Remembering
the Father of the Sky
and the Mother of the Earth.

Remembering
we are
passers-by on this beautiful journey
we who have
embodied our spirit are
the ones who are blessed.

Blessed are we by the
Heavens and the Earth
and
all the lives within
the light of our soul.

Ah!!! I thought
death was going to
be such a terrible
thing.

Now I rejoice
embrace
and love
all of who I am.

These special invitations
can only be received
with the joy of becoming.

With the joy of remembering.

With the joy of the gift
of Life.

Ah!
How sweet this
taste in my mouth.

A sweetness that
cannot even be described.

It is the sweetness of
being alive and breathing.

WISE WIND

The winds of change
blow
across the Prairies
the landscape
becomes a
white blanket
of snow
in the dead of
winter.

The wind whispers—

Listen!

Do you feel
Her soul reaching
out?

Listen!

Do you hear
Her words of
wisdom that
she brings from
the heavens?

Feel Her caresses
as She envelopes
all of your being.

Sometimes gentle
and smooth
for that is
what you need
at this time.

Other moments
you feel the harshness
of whirlwinds and
deep
transformational breath.

All is necessary,
the gentleness, the
harshness—

She knows—
Her Spirit is living
here on this
Earth.

She is one of the
Daughters of the
Earth.

Open your heart
to the glorious
Wind—
    She waits for you
    Every Day!!!

CYCLES

Time passes
we remain in
different forms.

Death is at your
door—Are you afraid?

Cycles of life
are irreversible,
we can only
invite them
ready
or not.

And your heart
Dear Father,
has been
broken for a
long time.

The voices of
your parents
are only a
breath away.

They call you
now from their
hearts.

The lineage continues.

Good-byes are said

And then—

Until we see each other when
we are together again.

Ci vediamo quando stiamo insieme!

THE HEART OF BEING

I have been wrestling
in my sleep
remembering vaguely
what I have dreamt.

Sometimes it feels like
I am wrestling demons,
or shadows that have
appeared
always a
sense of deep
tiredness and
at the same time
sadness
in my heart.

Like the breath—
a hanging on and
letting go.

Every time I go to sleep
I feel like death
is lurking
around the corner,
preparing
for a great
ceremony.

A ceremony where
everyone is waiting
and at the same time
no one is there.

This place is
so familiar
and yet,
I cannot wrap
my mind
around it.

It is definitely a
sign of the times.

Every second
every breath a
letting go,
deeper
into the
heart of being.

II
REMEMBERING

WIND

I feel
I have
lived for thousands
of years.

The spirit of
wind
reminds me of
these lives.

The wind
her spirit
speaks to me.

She blows
words
into my ears.

She caresses me.

I feel her
in my hair
and on my skin.

Mostly,
I feel her
walk with me.

Sometimes
in a gentle
and loving way.

Sometimes
in a rough
and seducing way.

I know there
were times
when I needed
her harshness.

Despite these times
her beauty and love
always shone through.

You, dearest wind
are truly a blessing.

Learning
from you
from your spirit.

Meeting
as one,
joining you
in my last breath.

I pray
each breath
I take
remembers
your spirit

May I always Walk
In Beauty!

THE WEB

The web of life
is like a tree
the leaves fall
and die away
but the spirit
of the tree remains.

It seems we have
forgotten
the change and
the balance of
things.

Even as I write
change occurs
the paper gets wet
from the falling
rain
the words that
flow from heart
to hand
create
a new web
or perhaps
a web which is
remembered.

The cells in my body
respond in awe

They take a
breath of
relief
nothing really stays the
same.

The heart knows
nature changes
as do we.

We shed
our skin so that
we too can walk
again
in an old
familiar way
a way from long
ago.

This time the
ancestors walk
through us.

Oh! Surely you
must know
they have returned
and
they have always
been here
whispering in
our ears

"Wake Up!"

"Wake Up!"

"Wake Up!"

"Wake Up!"

"It is time!"

"It is time!"

"It is time!"

"It is time!"
for the web to
move through
you in your
remembering.

EMBRACE OF THE WIND

The wind has travelled
many miles to be
with me.

Her soul that is!

I am blessed with
Her presence every day.

Sometimes I forget.
but She soon
reminds me—

Her soft embrace
as She makes her
way through the trees and
branches.

Her gentle touch as
She caresses my face
and gently moves my hair.

I feel her all around
me even if I am not
outside.

She has penetrated my
soul and my bones.

I am of Her and She
of me

We are one and
inseparable.

I honor Her as
She has honored me
always.

She is always present.

I feel Her
inside me when
it is time to
Wake Up!

With Her gentle
waves of Compassion
She places Her
hands inside my
heart.

I hear Her
voice—sometimes
like a whisper.

Wake Up! Wake Up!

Wake Up! Wake Up!

I come to
carry you to your
own deep remembering.

Oh! Dear One who has
lived for many thousands
of life times.

All is ready—Everything
has been prepared.

Now all you have to
do is step in!!!

Step In! Step In!

Step Into Your Life!

Step Into Your Life!

Step Into Your Life!

Step in.

SACRED LOVE

Dusk is upon
the sky
and
the loneliness
of my heart
cries out.

I feel the
sacredness
of what
it is
to love
another soul.

To love my
own soul
that I have
missed for
so long
is
both
an unfolding
and a becoming.

A remembering
of the sacred.

REMEMBERING

When you finally
come down
from the mountain
the spark
of the Creator
will
begin to manifest
in the physical body
every cell
will be
illuminated—
and the
remembering
will go
even deeper
than before.

It is as if
His hands
reach in
and hold
your heart
you can
remember
who you are
and why
you are here.

TALKING STICK

I have come from a
far away land

Even if you found
me here today
I am your teacher
I am your Grandmother and
Grandfather.

All I ask for is
that you
listen to the teachings
with your heart.

Remember,
I am the gift
of the
Great Mother the Earth.

Her cells vibrate
through me as
they vibrate
through you.

Respect, Honor and Listen.

Listen—
Listen—
Listen—

AT LAST

We arrive naked
in this world
from the other
world.

We cover ourselves
with mud so that
we can forget.

Then one day
upon awakening to
a different kind of
day,

We realize the
journey is to
remember how
we arrived
in the first
place.

AN END TO A NEW BEGINNING

I prepare
to go to sleep
this night,
the night before
the night of
the opening of
a new life.

A life
I can walk tall in,
a life
I am born to be in.

How blessed and
grateful I feel,
for this life and
the support
and guidance I have
to sustain it.

Despite all the chaos
around me, there is
a deep seated pearl
in my heart
which cannot
be moved.

Staying still and centered,
remain solid
and yet
flowing amongst
the strongest storm.

Tomorrow is the last day
and the first day
of the rest of my life.

My heart feels full of
joy, knowing I am leaving
a place that has served me.

With deep gratitude I leave,
and now the time has come
to remove the robe and
leave it behind.

I feel like the teacher
in the desert
that has been
with me as a vision
since last fall.

I see all the wisdom
the knowing
in her face—my face.

SOUL COMING HOME

Dearest little one
you have returned
I felt you were
so far away and
yet you were
only a breath
away.

Your big brown
eyes remind me
of innocence and
love.

You shine like
an angel
in heaven
like a star in
the vast galaxy.

You have returned!

You have returned!

I am blessed with
the fullness of your
love and freedom.

I am blessed with
your ever lasting
presence.

Gratefulness fills my
heart!!

Gratefulness fills my
Heart!!!!

BEAUTY MADE FLESH

My legs feel like
they've walked
a thousand miles.

There are days
when the breath
in my body
feels like the wind
on a cool spring day.

And my mind
wonders about
how ancient
I am
as ancient
as this Earth.

The Earth Mother
that sustains,
transforms and
changes with
each breath that
I take.

I can feel Her
heart beat
in mine—
the pounding of the
Ancient One.

Are we really
that different
from the Stars above,
the dust of the
Cosmos
and all that
is made of Earth?

Are we not all
made by the same
"Hand"
that has created
everything
that is
around us?

We are all One!

PRINCE EDWARD ISLAND

Here I am in a place
I've never been.

So familiar is
the Earth here,
red in color
with a distinct
character.

I feel the solidity
of the land
beneath my feet.

The deep silence
and auspiciousness
of the wind rustling
the leaves.

I can hear voices
from this land
Voices of the ancestors!

I stop and listen
I watch the wind
caress the trees
as the leaves flicker
in the dusk.

I am amazed
at this wondrous
Island P.E.I.
so majestic with
a deep rooted
sense of a time
long ago.

So much more to
say.
So much more to
see, feel, taste, experience—

Being here is
a breath of fresh air
a continuous sense
of life
running
through my veins.
Grateful for nature
Grateful for being alive!

The sun is setting now.

The day comes to an end.

REBORN FROM THE RED EARTH

The ocean with its
colored rocks and
sand dunes.

The color of
the red earth.

This land has
truly captured
my heart.

I feel a deep
kinship
here.

I now know what
the feeling of
belonging is.

It is the Earth
nature,
and all
that surrounds me.

How beautiful
simple
sacred
a place for deepening
one's own soul.

THE BREATH OF BEING

We sat for a long time
in silence.

There is a deep teaching
in me
about peacemaking

The prayer of each bead
is like every bead
in my blood,
every cell in my
body.

Speak the truth from
a time long ago.

The teachings are
embedded
in each of us.

A whisper in an ear,
a caress of the wind
upon wings of the
great birds.

The blood that runs
through our veins like
the waters that flow
on the Earth our Mother.

I listen to the whispers
I open my heart
Spirit fills me with
His light of becoming
swirls around me
becoming the
wings of an Eagle.

The words flow and
they stop,
a stirring occurs
and more words
flow.

What a beautiful process
my life
my unique rhythm
each single time
my heart beats.

I listen—I feel full
with the light of Spirit
as I watch
the dance and union
with my own light
and with the breath
of becoming.

THE MOTH

Watching a moth
trying to penetrate
the light.

Never giving up
continuing to
flap her wings.

Then she stops,
is filled with
illumination.

Her seeking is
relentless,
her spirit strong.

The singing angels
allows her to glow.

The light
drawing her
to the sound of Spirit
calling her home.

Not knowing if it
is her time, she
continues
in the light
finding
that she
has come out
of the darkness.

III
RE-BIRTH

FLESH

The body,
the physical part
of the being

The part that is
flesh and bones.

How Sacred
is the flesh?

The flesh born
from star dust
and particles
tumbling down
onto this great planet

Mother Earth!

The bones encoded
with millions
of years of evolution,
before we walked
the Earth
before we existed
before our own birth.

We are made
Sacred—
this flesh we Honor

As we Honor
the flesh
all becomes
blessed,
pure and Holy.

Flesh made alive
from the Breath
of the Creator
which surrounds
us like the wind.

We cannot
see the Sacred
but we
feel it
in and around the
flesh.

We know it—always.

SPRING

The snow is
soft and fresh
like cotton
falling
from the sky.

The trees are
caressed
like
new born babies
on a winter day.

Snow blankets
cover the trees
as they
wake up
from a deep
winter sleep.

Warmth within
waiting—
to stretch
and grow leaves
for the Spring.

The cycle continues
and I see myself
in the center
of this wheel
surrounded
by the wonderful
change of life.

I stand in the center
following the wheel
one step at a time.

Cycles, change—

Life—
Death—
Rebirth!

SACRED PEACE

The spiral dance
has begun.

I am the
spiral dance.

Eagles come to
dance
wing to wing
in the Sky.

Seeing the whole
—the Soul

Coming together in
the spiral—
Soul and Body—Sacred One!

My heart speaks
of a profound
knowing.

My mind dissolves.

My soul
pulses
in growth,
as large as
the universe—
larger than
the life I imagined
for myself.

Every cell
in my body sparkling
with the knowing
of each moment
as it unfolds.

I know why
I have come to
this Great Mother Earth!

I am here
to bring **Peace**
in a Sacred Way.

In the way
that
the ancient ones
have been waiting for.

The way is deep
in my cells
and in my DNA.

I can hear the call—
the sound,
the vibration.

The call
    listen, listen!

The Ancestors are
calling
you, too!

THE WAIT IS OVER

The wobble begins
in my heart.

The energy spirals
up to my head
and down,
all the way down into
my feet.

It is like being
a top,
spinning
round and round
while the center
is stable.

The challenge
is not to fall
but to allow
the deep rooted
sense of trust
and faith
to remain.

Ah!
My longing
is so strong.

The longing—for
Peace!

The Vision of Peace!

All over the world
my circle of people
being manifested

The time is
NOW!

To act—To create!

Time to Come Out
of hiding.

The waiting is over.

Time to get Moving.

Act
I am
The Activist.

I am
who
I have been waiting for.

THE PULSE OF MY HEART

I feel a burning desire
in my heart.

As I get closer
to the fire
I can feel a pulsing.

The pulse of my
heart,
the pulse of the
Earth.

The fire has been
burning for centuries.

It is time to put
the wood in,
to allow the ashes
to become specks.

These are the ashes
of my soul.

The ashes of my
longing.

The ashes of Peace!

THE TIME IS NOW

With every beginning
there really is no
end.

My life, my relationships
are woven into new
webs
every moment
of every day.

Stepping aside
I allow
the weaving
to weave me too.

Surely my life
can only continue
to evolve,
shift and change form.

The questions are:

Where do I go from here?

How can I be an instrument of
change?

The voice inside
keeps getting louder!

"Activist
bring
social change"

Where to begin?

Is it a dance,
a spiral,
an ever ending web
that continues
for millennia!

Enough questions!

Time to act and do.

Time to begin
time to continue
the work that
has been here.

The work begun
by those who have
walked before me.

How can I honour
those that have
come before me?

Those that are
waiting to be
born?

Open your eyes!

I will open my eyes,
I will allow myself
to be seen.

I feel a deep longing,
this is the way.

My heart opens,
there is
no turning back.

THE WEB OF LIFE

Days full and rich
with all things
imaginable.

I sit and reflect
upon the beauty
of being alive.

What an opportunity?

A blessing—life

Tomorrow we come
together once more

We will laugh, cry,
sing and dance together.

The beauty of who each
one is will be
present.

This web of life
fills my heart
with gratitude,
for every single soul
that sits around
this circle.

It is being in the
presence of
Kings and Queens.

Precious souls that have
touched my heart so deeply.

I leave with such a richness

It is like brownies
and the ice cream.
rich, sweet, delicious,
always leaving
a deep longing
for wanting
more.

BRAVA!

I waited 46 years to hear
that word
that the child in me
did not hear often.

And
you who has
such honour and grace
uttered them without
hesitation.

For that I feel a welling up
of tears,
a kind of relief
occurs in my body.

This little one inside
is so grateful that
the word has come
from you.

Thank You!

THE WHEEL OF LIFE

The wheel
continues to turn me,
in ways that
are both profound
and eye opening
Spirit is always
attentive
and present.

THE BLESSING OF LIFE

This past week
has been like
a blink of an eye.

It seems like
people I know
or have known
come from
far away.

Sometimes
change and
other things
stay the same.

Is there a constant?

Yes, of course—

CHANGE!!!!!!

Our lives take on
a new light

We grow older,
physically but
wiser in spirit
and heart.

Sometimes it feels like
a gust of wind
brings
old memories
and at other times
it feels like
a breath of fresh air.

IMPRINT

I am surrounded
by grief
in my own life
and all those
around me also
are deep in
their own grief
of divorce, illness,
and letting go
of youth as we
move into our
middle age.

What kind of
mark are we
making?

What do we
leave behind
as we enter
the second half
of our life?

We all make a mark
no matter
how big or
small.

So blessed to be alive!

THE SACRED LABYRINTH

Step
into your life.
The life you
have known
since the beginning
of time.

Step
by step
feeling
the Earth support you.

Step
by step
allow
the swirling wind
to embrace you.

Step
by step
the sacred
enters
your heart.

The blanket of being
falls upon your
shoulders.

A gentle warmth
enters your
body and
the darkness of
the night
becomes light
and the light
is infused
by dark.

Step
by step
possibilities
arise.

Step
by step
the light of
your soul is
ignited.

Step
by step
you know
you have come home
once more to yourself.

MEDITATION

The brightest golden light
surrounds her body
like a blanket of
shimmering gold.

Her hair reflects
the light against
the wall around
her,
the deepest parts
of herself exposed.

Radiant she is!
So radiant, like
the holy goddess
holding a babe
in her arms.

The baby sleeps
feeling the blessing
love and trust of
his holy Mother!

And then as she
moves
I realize
she is really
holding herself.

BUILDING THE BRIDGE OF PEACE

For so long I have been
searching,
and all along it was
right in front of me.

My vision was set
on a far away place,
a place with some
familiar notion
about how life should be.

And then as if
for the first time
I opened the door
that dwelled
deep inside my
heart,
and I knew it
was time to allow
the teachings to come
pouring through.

It is time
to continue to build
the bridge.

The bridge has been
left unattended
for too long,
the building resumes
and what I have known
for so long
can be brought
forth into the world.

UNFOLDING

Nothing to write
the mind is empty
and full at the same
time.

The silence brings
waves of buzzing
in my ears—
my eyes can see
further
than I thought
possible.

My body
feels the peace
of the Earth and also its
transformation
as it gets ready
to burst into
Spring.

The answers—
they are here
they will come
when the
heart
is so ripe
and ready
to burst
out of the
chest.

And then
I am still
left with
the
silence
and
the deep
knowing
of a new
beginning.

A new life
ready
to unfold
with each new
season,
with every
breath
I see
a blank page
ready to be
filled or
not.

Sometimes
the words
come
in the waiting
time.

Sometimes they are
at my finger
tips
and I know
I have been
ignoring them.

And then a
voice
appears,
so gentle,
so loving,
like a caress
from the Wind
and
I hear:
Your heart has
all the answers—

Listen!

And I know
that although
my life feels
like it is ending—

My life is just
beginning.

FOUNDATION

I see a new chapter
in my life unfolding
like the branches
of the Great White Pine Tree,
rooted deep into the Earth
and reaching
up into the great
vast Sky.

The foundation solid
the wind comes
embraces me
and then moves on.

A foundation built
on peace is never
broken.

It may shift, sway
and get bent out of
shape.

But before I know it
a new form arises
and the foundation
becomes stronger.

What a great gift
to have deep in my heart,
a gift
from the Creator
who whispers
in my ear when I
have forgotten

"Continue to build
the bridge, the
young ones are
coming."

LIFE

Life
is more than a vision
of the outside world.

Life is a vision of
the inside world.

When we see the
inside and the infinite
possibilities
the outside can be reflected
by each and every one
of us.

The reflections of our
soul will create
peace and healing in
the world.

We have all arrived!

DEEPENING

It is in the deep
silence
of all things,
this place
where manifestation
occurs.

From a deep
darkness
emerges a
new life.
A familiar
life
one we
remember from
another time,
a time
where all
was born
from nothing
and yet
as we know
this
we also
struggle
through each
growing pain,
each breath.

LETTING GO

I feel a deep
sense of loss
in my body.

I feel like I've
been turned
inside out.

Nothing is familiar
anymore!

I look around and
everything looks
shiny, sparkling,
new!

I feel both
a sense of awe
and at the same time
confusion.

This new
and familiar
place

I have been
here before
and I am
beginning to
remember as
if
I am here
in this body
for the
very first
time!

IV
COMING HOME

SO YOUNG

I walked with you
a whole year,
not knowing
the outcome.

As you prepared
to cross the threshold
of death
I was honored
to watch
and hold you.

I still feel a
deep sadness
in my heart.

So young and
beautiful you left
the Earth on golden
wings.

Such a bright
and vibrant soul
even your cells
were shaped
like stars.

I WILL WALK WITH YOU

I will take your hand
and go where ever you
need to go.

I will walk with you
to the end of time
where the stillness
of life lives.

I will witness every
step you take
as the path emerges.

I will walk with you
to the gate of
everlasting love.

There we shall
say our goodbyes
as you continue
your walk alone.

A FAR AWAY PLACE

I have arrived
from a far away
place.

This place feels
familiar and yet
strange.

I could not
have imagined
this life for
myself.

I only dreamt
about it
and now like
a waking dream
I have stepped
fully into
the unity of
my selves,

I feel a deep
embrace inside
my heart.

It feels like
an embrace
from the
universe.

It feels like
I am surrounded
by the spirits
of my ancestors.

They are all
clapping—

Can you hear them!

MIRROR

I see the
love in your
eyes
not realizing
that I was
looking at
myself.

SACRED MEDICINE WHEEL

I lay upon
the Earth,
my spine
glued to the ground
I lay between
East and North
within the
Sacred Medicine
Wheel.

My heart ached
with some sort
of longing and
then
I sank
deep
into the
Earth
into the
darkness
of death.

I reached
the center
the burning
center of
the Great
Mother.

I went up
in flames
I saw myself
as a baby
and then as
I grew
I lifted
myself up
from the
center of the Earth
a great cloak of
white feathers
surrounded me.

The ancestors
smiling, joyful,
rejoicing.

I moved
through and
above and then
upon the wings
of the great
Eagle I am
transported
through the
Sun.

As I moved
through the
fire
the Sun
engulfed me and
I became
transformed
again.

I watch in awe
and just as
I think it's
over I
come across
my home—
my Star planet.

The Elders are
waiting,
as I approach
they begin
anointing me
with a
special feather
one by one.

Far in the distance
a great Elder
appears with
an Eagle feather.

As he approaches
I can feel my heart
beat speeding up.

When I can finally
see Him I see
my father in this
life,
I begin to cry.

He blows into
my third eye and
into my heart.

He adorns me
with the feather
smiles
and moves on.

The drum begins
to call us back.
I make my
way back to
the Earth.

I feel a deep
transformation.

I feel grateful!

I step out of the
Medicine Wheel
and give my thanks.

I return with the
teaching embedded
deep in my heart.

CHAMBER OF LIFE

My belly is
like a lava pit
boiling inside
bubbling up
waiting patiently
to arise
waiting patiently
to be noticed
awakening to the
channel
the central tunnel
the central channel
leading to
the chambers
the chambers
of the brain

The remembering
the awakening
the knowledge
comes pouring
out.

Exposed, grateful is
what I feel
and I sit here
and write and there
are no more
words.

HEART TO HEART

I awake to
the chirping of
birds

The Sun rises
and a new day
begins

Every day a
new beginning,
every day an
opportunity
to remember

I take a deep
breath
I allow all
the cells in
my body
to wake up!

I will not go
back to sleep

My body is
rested and
yet my cells vibrate
with a new
awakening with
each breath
I take.

Each breath
a deepening
each breath
a remembering!

Time to move
my body—
Nature is
calling me.

She is inviting
me to be
with her heart.

Heart to heart
we speak
and sit
together.

BLESSING

I awake
to the singing
birds.

What beautiful
music to tickle
my eardrums
with.

The Sun shines
through my window.

My heart is full
with the connection
of this beautiful
Earth

The differences
have disappeared
and all that is
left is the
blessing of the
Creator!

WHITE PINE

I sit on a bench
within a symphony
of birds
at Columcille.

I am being held
by two beautiful
white pine trees.

As I look
in front of me
a tiny white pine
looks back.

I can feel the
youngness of
her heart and
her excitement
to grow.

She already has
a huge heart,
ready to embrace
and allow
the Spirit of the wind
to move
through her.

How beautiful
it is to watch
someone grow!

There are no
more words
just the beauty
of silence.

In my heart I
feel honored to
be able to witness
such beauty and grace.

RED TAIL HAWK

I watch you fly
across the sky
like an old
dream,
I call out to
you to come
closer and
to my surprise
you do
I feel honored
by your presence
and blessed
knowing you are
here

You fly high
in the sky so
that you can
have vision
you can see
all of what
you need from
up there.

And then I
realize
that I can see
all of what
I need too!

STEP IN

We must not
sit still
anymore!

We must act!

Being complacent
is just an
excuse or
fear turned
inside out
by the mind.

We all want
peace and yet
we sit and
wait
for what,
I do not
know.

Time passes and
each one of
us needs to
step up.

Our desires
are living deep
in our hearts.

Please unlock
the door
step in.

Allow the
magic to
become a
blanket of
Peace.

WITH OPEN ARMS

I have no
more words
death is
approaching
and all I
hear is
the rustling
of leaves,
the wind
and the
call of
the ancestors
saying—

"Come Home,
it is time.
We are waiting with
open arms
and with the
golden light
of the Great
Mystery."

It is time to
join with us
to continue
your journey
in this
world
The Spirit World."

The physical
part dies
to make
good compost
for the Great
Mother the
Earth
but
the spirit
grows and will
continue to
grow.

NO MORE WORDS

Everything feels
still and quiet
even though I
can hear the
morning doves
and the wind.

What is silence?

Even in the void
there is sound and
all of my senses
are awake.

I feel a deep
wisdom in my heart
like a knowing
it feels old and
I cannot put
words to what
this feeling is.

Somehow I trust
that when the
words are ready
they will adorn
a white page
waiting for me
to put pen to paper

and yet

there is a place
inside of me that
feels like the
page will remain
as white as the
bright light of the
journey home
not words just
light.

THE FOUNTAIN

The angels have
spread their
wings
the golden light
of the Creator
is shining upon
you,
the way is before
you, Dad.

When you are
ready just ask
and the angels will
guide you upon
their wings of
love and light.

The way is prepared—
look at the
path towards the
fountain you
so love

The fountain which
holds the drink
of eternal life
in the arms
of the Creator.

The wings
await beyond
the fountain

What a glorious
journey you are
taking,
I am
honored,
privileged
to walk
beside you.

Thank you for this
gift of
witnessing
you
in transition
from life
on Earth
to life
in Heaven.

DISSOLVING

It seems like
as my father
prepares to
die
I prepare
to step into
my life,
the old way or
the old role
of daughter
dissolves
somehow.

Something new
is created
I know it
in my bones.

I cannot tell
you exactly
what it is yet.

All I can
say is this:

The tightness
has loosened
I feel more
peaceful
and
fear dissolves
even more.

SPIRIT

The process
is simple
everything
we have known
in a physical way
dissolves.

The body is
infused with
Spirit.

EMERGING

It is in preparing
to die
that I see
you come
alive.

As I watch you,
Dear Father,
preparing
for your journey
back to
the source
of all life
that I
feel blessed
with your
full
life.

Your personality
continues to
dissolve and
the light
of who you
are
emerges.

I know it
is your
soul
and yet
I feel a
deep
sadness
in my
heart.

I ask myself
Why is it
through death
that light
emerges?

A part of me
knows the
answers and
a part of
me feels
empty of all
the years
I missed
knowing you
in this way.

Gratefulness
fills my heart
with this
opportunity
to walk with
you and to
know you
once more
for who
you really
are.

I love you, Dad.

ALONE

I've never felt
this way before
adrenaline
rushing in my
body,
incredible
heat.

I feel so
alone here
on this airplane
going north,
home to
Montreal.

I am realizing
in these
few moments
of my life
that I
do not
have to
be good
or strong
or stoic.

It's O.K.
for me to
be afraid
alone and out
of control,
overwhelmed.

These times
are truly
challenging.

My emotions
feel like a
whirlwind
in my heart
and part of me
is confused.

I know,
as my father
prepares to
die
I am
questioning
my own
mortality,
life feels
shorter
than I
thought and

there is
so much
to do, see,
and be.

I miss Sue,
I guess
that's what
this is,
we are
getting closer
and closer
and it is
becoming
harder and harder
being apart.

Writing relaxes
me and
calms me,
once the words
are out on paper
I feel like
I can breath
again.

I feel so
grateful for
my life on
this Earth
no matter
how long,

It is a
privilege, honor
and duty to
be walking upon
the Great Mother
the Earth.

COMING HOME

As I look
out
the back door
onto the garden
my mind
travels back to
the past.

I hear children
playing—me and my sisters.
Mom and Dad
laughing.

The tomato
sauce is cooking,
it smells
like heaven,
the joy of food—pasta.

The Sunday morning
ritual,
these memories
seem so
far away and yet
they are right here
in this moment.

Even though death
lurks possibly just
moments away,
maybe hours, days,
or months.

It is out of my
hands and yet
I stand, witness,
feel the suffering
of the present
illness eating
away at my father.

I know that
there is more
than that,
years and years and
centuries of suffering
are in his bones.

As he prepares
to die
the suffering
heightens and
then subsides and the
beautiful shiny soul
that he is continues
to emerge.

This blessing,
this glorious sight
it is like witnessing
a new life somehow
a life preparing the
way.

Making a mark.

A light emerging
amongst all the
others.

The light of
my ancestors.

It seems so
perfect—this
process,
so natural.

Then
the mind
steps in to
deny the truth
possibly but
the heart speaks
louder:

Let go
step out of the
way.

Come Home!

Come Home!

SWEET LIFE

When the cold
comes
I will whither
away
like the leaves
on
a tree.

The North
Wind
guides
my journey
to
the ancestors
who
wait
patiently.

I surrender
my body
to the
Earth.

My Spirit
soars
toward
the
heavens.

How sweet
the taste of
this life
on this
Earth.

What is even
sweeter
is the
water
that
waits for me
at the fountain
of a new life.

A life of
returning home
finally
in the
arms
of the
Creator.

BREATH

I sit here
beside you,
dear Dad,
and I watch
your breath.

Your breath,
is like the
wind
which enters
each soul
to give it
life.

As death
approaches
with one
last breath
we
reunite
with the
wind.

The breath
of the cosmos.

I feel a
certain
freedom and
liberation
in my
heart.

Even as
the physical
dissolves
there is
peace
upon
your face.

The personality
and the ego
shows its face,

but
when you
sleep
you look
peaceful
aware
once more
of your
connection
with the Creator.

REUNITED

Denial is
the trickster
of humankind.

What we deny
we do not
embrace.

To deny death
is to deny life.

For death is a
blessing in itself.

It is like the
caress of the
wind or the
rustling of
leaves,
the cry of
a baby,
the embrace
of love
and
the union
of a soul
with the
Creator.

TRANSITION

No words
to describe
this feeling.

Loss.

My heart
feels bruised
like an
apple that
has fallen,
hard
upon the Earth.

At the same
time my heart
has never felt
so open
so full
full of love
full of compassion.

This is a deep and
profound initiation
for me
into the world
of no words
and the infinite
light of the
Creator—

In the next
breath,
I move into
the world of
words and my
physical life
on Earth.

I am still
in transition
still looking and
searching for
clarity somehow
but I don't
know if it
will ever come.

Death has a
way of bringing
change whether
I like it
or not

If
I can see all
the goodness of
this I know
I will be filled
with even more
good medicine
in order to live
an even fuller
life.

THE JOURNEY HOME

As I watch
you die
I see your
heart open
more and more
a vessel is
created from
your heart
to way above
your head.

The angels have
created a dome
of light in order
for you—Dad
to move back
and forth and through
and they are all
waiting.

When you are
ready the
golden umbilicus
attached to
your crown
will carry you
to the Creator
to the infinite
light of all.

I have been
accompanying
you and I
have waited
at the gate
and soon there
will be no
more waiting.

Your spirit
will soar
into the
Divine light
and you will
be free.

I feel honoured
and blessed to
be on this
journey with
you.

The last trip
will be on
your own
with the
Angels and

we will say our
good-byes
at the gate
and until we
see each other
when
we are together again.

You have
prepared
the way.

INVITATION

The end feels
near and yet
it also feels
far away.

The cancer
is eating
away at
you, Dad.

I pray for
peace in
your heart
and soul.

The physical
dissolves
the soul
remains
we know
this in our
bones.

To invite
death is
to invite
all of our
Ancestors
to the table
of life.

Here, Dad,
you will
eat from
the table
of everlasting
life.

Your journey
has created
a path for
all of us to
follow when
the time comes.

I will follow
with great
honour knowing
you have
made the way.

SACRED CIRCLE

My heart
filled as I
heard
the voices
of my
ancestors.

I knew I
had to
listen!

Somehow in
the Sacred
circle your
words are
also my words.

To see
the ancient
ones whisper in
my ears
was a profound delight.

I watched
myself
speak the
words and I
allowed myself
to hear their
whispers.

I allowed
myself to
speak the
truth
and in the speaking,
with a heart
full of love,
I was able
to finally
see myself.

HOME

So here we
are,
we meet again
you with the
heart of the
Great Mother
I have honoured
you since
the time before
time.

We come together
to remember
to speak
to act
to gather
like we did
before.

All is familiar
at this time
in this place.

This place
Mt. Eden which
feels like
home once
more.

And I ask
myself: Where
on this Earth
do I not feel
at home?

My answer is:
I feel at home
everywhere as
long as I am
home with
myself.

SACRED TRANSITION

To know death
in our bones
is to know
life in our
hearts.

The sacred
transition
from life
into death
is one of
the greatest
rites of
passage.

The mind
hangs on
for dear
life.

But it is
in the
letting go
that we
begin to see
the light.

The light has
always been
there, but—
we have been
blinded
by our
addictive
mind.

Then when death
knocks on
our door
we receive
the gift
of allowing
all of our
personality
and ego to
dissolve and—

What is left?

Our luminescent light!

Our Soul!

SPACE

I do not feel a
need to rush off
to the hospital.

A deep trust has
deepened within me.

It doesn't really
matter whether I
am there in person
or not, I know
we are together.

Somehow the curtain
has been drawn and
the veil between
this world and the
next has disappeared.

I feel no need
to hang on to the
past or to the
future toward what
might be.

All I feel in this
very moment is
space, space, space.

And when everything
dissolves
all that really remains is
Love.

HOME AT LAST

The tears we
are shedding will
wash away the
pain.

Each tear will
make its way
into our hearts
in order to
create a dear
memory of your
love for us.

And when the
wind blows
your voice
will be
added to
the ones of
our ancestors.

We will listen
carefully to
your wisdom
dearest Dad.

When the moon
shines bright
into the night

the memory of
your teachings
will be present.

The sun will
remind us of
your beloved
Italy
the town
you were born
in, Casacalenda
and the dry heat
of the country you
came from.

Now you live
in all the
elements around
us.

You walk with us
upon the Sacred Earth.

We feel you in a
drink of water.

In the fire we use
to heat our food
and our bones.

In the air we breath
and in the space you
hold for us in the
Spirit world.

You have
prepared the
way!

You have
prepared the
way!

Your life as well
as your dying process
has been a gift
to us all.

ABOUT THE AUTHOR

Rosa Bergola is a poet, storyteller, healer, lecturer, spiritual counselor, and teacher. She is a Holistic Health Practitioner trained in indigenous process work, ceremony, energy medicine, counseling, guided imagery, conflict resolution, and peacemaking. She is a Peacemaker Minister, Dean and founder of The Peacemaker School of Canada. Since 1994 she has been devoted to a professional healing practice in Montreal, Quebec, Canada working with individuals as well as with groups. She teaches classes on ceremony, meditation, chakras, energy medicine, grief as a divine journey, hands-on-healing, and peacemaking.

Rosa can be reached via e-mail at rosa@bellnet.ca, phone 514-251-1511, toll free 1-866-251-1511, or by mail at 5964 de Jumonville, #5, Montreal, Quebec H1M 1R3 Canada.

THE PEACEMAKER SCHOOL OF CANADA

The Peacemaker School of Canada is a bilingual non-profit, ecumenical, spiritual and educational organization. Our mission is to foster peace, healing and community building in the world through teaching, embodying and practicing peacemaking skills.

These teachings encompass, but are not limited to: prayer, meditation, conflict resolution, spiritual practices, environmental practices, traditional laying-on-of-hands, energy medicine, community building, creative arts, insight and awareness training, ceremony, ethics and activism.

FOR MORE INFORMATION:

The Peacemaker School of Canada

Rosa Bergola
Dean and Founder
5964 de Jumonville, #5,
Montreal, Quebec
H1M 1R3
Canada
514-251-1511
1-866-251-1511
rosa@bellnet.ca

The Peacemaker School USA

Jane Ely
Dean and Co-Founder
Lihue, Kauai, HI
808-245-4246

Self Publishing

Christina Manolescu
1192 Egan Street, Verdun
Quebec, Canada
(01) 514-807-4171
christina@princechameleon.com
Invisible Cities Network
www.InvisibleCitiesNetwork.org

Marquis Book Printing Inc.

Québec, Canada
2009